Can't I Just Be Like Everyone Else?
How to Fit In, Speak Up, and Handle Life Without Faking It

Jennifer Larsen

Copyright © 2025 by Jennifer Larsen

All rights reserved. No part of this book may be reproduced, stored in a retrieval system, or transmitted in any form or by any means, electronic, mechanical, photocopying, recording, or otherwise without the prior written permission of the publisher, except in the case of brief quotations used in reviews, articles, or educational settings.

This book is a work of nonfiction intended to provide general guidance. It is not a substitute for professional advice. The author has made every effort to ensure the accuracy and completeness of the information contained herein, but assumes no responsibility for errors, omissions, or differing interpretations.

Originality Statement

This book is an original work written by the author and reflects their unique ideas, voice, and instructional approach. While it may reference common educational and career-planning concepts, all content, including structure, language, exercises, and framework, is the author's own creation. Any similarities to other published works are purely coincidental.

Printed in the United States of America

ISBN: 979-8-9987626-9-7

First Edition

Cover design by Rachel Bostwick

Interior design and layout by Rachel Bostwick

For information or bulk orders, visit cantijust.com

Can't I Just Be Like Everyone Else?
How to Fit In, Speak Up, and Handle Life Without Faking It

📖 Introduction:
You're Not Broken – You're Just Untranslated 1

📖 Chapter 1:
First Impressions and The Art of
Not Accidentally Looking Like a Menace 7

📖 Chapter 2:
Facial Expressions – Why "This Is Just My Face"
Might Still Get You Detention 19

📖 Chapter 3:
Tone, Volume, and the Magical Skill of Not Sounding Rude 29

📖 Chapter 4:
Texts, Chats, and Social Media –
Soft Skills Go Digital 41

📖 Chapter 5:
Apologizing Like a Real Person (Not a Scripted Robot) 51

📖 Chapter 6:
Group Work, Teachers, and Being Assertive 61

📖 Chapter 7:
Social Rules That Aren't in the Handbook 73

📖 Chapter 8:
Emotional Self-Control (Without Going Numb or Exploding) 83

📖 Chapter 9:
Being a Decent Human Without Overdoing It 93

📖 Chapter 10:
Soft Skills at Work (or Work-Like Places) 103

📖 Closing Chapter:
You Don't Have to Be a Genius – You Just Have to Be Aware 113

📖 Glossary: Soft Skills Decoder 121

📖 Soft Skills Survival Cheat Sheet
(Quick Phrases, Real Strategies) 125

📖 Introduction:
You're Not Broken
– You're Just Untranslated

Let's get one thing straight right away:

This book is not here to fix you.

You're not broken.

You're not rude on purpose.

You're not "too intense" or "too quiet" or "too anything."

You're just... sometimes misunderstood.

And that's where soft skills come in.

💡 Wait. What Even Are Soft Skills?

"Soft skills" are the non-academic, non-technical, completely human things that people expect you to know – but rarely explain.

They're the reason you can say something totally normal and still get in trouble.

They're the reason a teacher might think you're "not trying," or a classmate thinks you "have an attitude," even when you don't.

They're also the reason some people just seem to get along with everyone, get picked for stuff, or get trusted right away.

It's not that they're better than you.

They just speak a language you might not have learned yet.

🫠 The Soft Skill Struggle Is Real

Here's what might be true about you:

- You say things directly, and people think you're rude.
- You look bored when you're actually focused.
- You get called disrespectful when you're just... tired.
- You don't like small talk, group work, or pretending to care about things you don't.

Cool. That's all valid.

But here's the problem: people are constantly **reading** you.

Even when you're not saying anything.

Even when you're doing your best.

And when they misread you, you can end up misunderstood, left out, or labeled.

That's not fair. But it *is* real.

So instead of pretending you're someone you're not, this book is going to teach you how to **translate yourself** into something people can understand – without losing your personality, values, or chill.

🎯 You Don't Have to Be Fake – Just Strategic

You don't need to smile 24/7.

You don't need to be super social.

You don't need to say "yes" to everything or be the group project leader.

You just need to know:
- What your face is saying when you're zoning out
- What your voice sounds like when you're stressed
- How your texts come across when you're trying to be chill but actually seem annoyed
- What to do when you mess up (because you will, and that's fine)

That's what this book is for.

🛠 How to Use This Book

- You can read it straight through or skip around.
- Every chapter includes examples, tips, and things you can *actually try*.
- Some parts will feel familiar. Some might make you go, "Oh... that's what happened that time."
- No guilt. No lectures. Just tools.

If something doesn't feel like "you," skip it. Or come back later.

This is your survival guide for people stuff.

For school. For friends. For work. For life.

For looking like you know what you're doing, even when you kinda don't.

Let's start translating.

📖 Chapter 1:
First Impressions and The Art of Not Accidentally Looking Like a Menace

You walk into a room.

You're tired. Maybe anxious. Or just trying to get through the day without getting called on.

And someone says it:

"What's with the attitude?"

Awesome.

The truth is, when you're a teen, people assume things about you.

They assume you're mad.

They assume you're uninterested.

They assume you don't care – even when you *do*.

That's because first impressions are loud.

And they often come from stuff you don't even realize you're doing.

So let's break down the art of **not accidentally scaring people off.**

◆ Why First Impressions Happen Fast (and Stick)

People make decisions about you in the first **seven seconds** of seeing you.

They look at your:

- **Face** (Are you smiling? Blank? Scowling?)
- **Posture** (Slouched? Upright? Tense?)
- **Energy** (Calm? Closed off? Intense?)
- **Eyes** (Avoiding? Staring? Wandering?)
- **Tone** (Even the way you say "hi" matters)

They don't wait to ask who you are.

They make a mental guess – and then everything you do after that filters through it.

If they guess "rude," you'll have to work twice as hard to seem kind.

If they guess "unreliable," your hard work might get ignored.

Is that fair? No.

Is it fixable? Absolutely.

- **So... Do I Have to Fake Being Friendly?**

Nope. But you do need to **be aware of what you're putting out there**.

This doesn't mean being bubbly or fake-smiling your way through the day.

It means asking yourself, *"Am I showing people what I actually want them to see?"*

You can be quiet and still seem kind.

You can be tired and still seem respectful.

You can be yourself and still come across the way *you want to* – once you learn the signals.

◆ The Signals You're Already Sending

Without saying a word, you might be telling people:

- "Don't talk to me."
- "I don't want to be here."
- "I'm better than this."
- "I'm totally lost."
- "I need help, but please don't look at me."

Even if you don't feel that way.

So here's how to **reclaim the first impression** without selling your soul.

✦ Try This: The Walk-In Check (Solo or Group)

Practice walking into a space (your bedroom, a classroom, anywhere) while imagining:

- You're being introduced to someone important
- You're arriving at a group project
- You're walking into a job interview (yes, even if that's years away)

Now check yourself:

- What are your arms doing?
- Are you looking up? Down? At your phone?
- What's your expression?
- How fast are you moving?

Now try it again, but this time:

- Keep your head up (not high, just level)
- Relax your face – try a soft, neutral mouth, not tight lips
- Uncross your arms or take your hands out of your pockets
- Walk at a normal pace, not rushed or dragging

Feels weird? That's normal.

Looks more confident? Absolutely.

💀 Quick Tip: Tired Face ≠ Bad Attitude

You're not a bad person because your face sags when you're tired.

But if you know your "neutral face" comes across as annoyed, you can *choose* to shift it when it matters.

Think of it like a **setting you can toggle**:

- "Normal Face" = default
- "Friendly Mode" = neutral eyes, relaxed mouth, body open
- "Shield Mode" = reserved posture, no expression
- "Help Me" = wide eyes, slight nod, soft tone

This isn't pretending – it's **positioning.**

You're saying, "Here's how I want to be read."

🎯 Try This Together: Vibe Check Challenge

In a group or pair, take turns doing short "walk-ins" while the other person guesses the vibe:

- Nervous
- Confident
- Closed off
- Friendly
- Fake friendly
- Trying not to cry (it happens)

Then talk about:

- What made it clear?
- What confused you?
- What would you change if that was a real situation?

This shows how powerful body language and tone are – and how fast people react to it.

Flip the Script: My First Impression Moment

Think of a time someone misread you.

Maybe they thought you were mad, rude, lazy, or didn't care – when you actually did.

Write or reflect:

- What were you doing with your body, face, or voice?
- How could you keep being *you*, but show your true intentions more clearly?
- What would you try if you could redo that moment?

What to Remember

- First impressions are fast and sticky – but you *can* guide them.
- You don't need to be fake, but you do need to check the signals you're giving off.
- Your face, posture, and energy can say "I care" even when your words are few.
- You get to choose your "default settings" – and tweak them when it matters most.

🔋 Mini Social Reality Check!

People *will* make snap judgments about you.

But here's the good news:

You're not stuck with the first one.

You can update the vibe. Reintroduce yourself through your actions. Prove people wrong.

And sometimes? That's kind of satisfying.

📖 **Chapter 2:
Facial Expressions –
Why "This Is Just My Face"
Might Still Get You Detention**

Let's talk about one of the most unfair, most frustrating things that happens to teens:

"Why are you glaring at me?"

You: *"…I'm literally just sitting here."*

Or:

- "Watch your attitude."
- "You're being disrespectful."
- "Don't roll your eyes at me." (Even if you didn't.)

There's a reason this happens, and no – it's not because your face is rude.

It's because **people rely on facial expressions to read what you mean**, and sometimes your face is saying things you didn't authorize.

So let's fix the signal without changing the system.

◆ The Face Doesn't Always Match the Feeling

You might be:

- **Zoning out** and look bored
- **Stressed** and look angry
- **Trying to stay calm** and look smug
- **Paying attention** and still somehow get accused of "glaring"

Why? Because your face has its own habits – and sometimes they don't match your actual mood.

This doesn't mean your face is wrong.

It just means it's *loud*, and you might want to check what it's saying.

- **People Read Micro-Expressions. (Yes, That's a Real Thing.)**

Micro-expressions are tiny movements in your face that happen fast and often without you realizing:

- A slight eye-roll
- A tiny eyebrow lift
- A quick lip twitch
- A mouth that tightens for half a second

Adults, especially teachers and supervisors, are trained – *without realizing it* – to pick up on these things.

Even if you didn't mean it.

So now they're responding to the "attitude" your face flashed for a microsecond, and you're left confused, annoyed, or in trouble.

Let's change the pattern.

🛠 Try This: Mirror Time – Expression Check

In front of a mirror or selfie cam, try these challenges:

1. Your "I'm listening" face
2. Your "I'm focused" face
3. Your "I'm chill" face
4. Your "I'm annoyed but trying to hide it" face
5. Your default resting face (just sit normally)

Ask yourself:
- What does each one look like to someone else?
- Would a stranger know what mood you're in?
- Does your focused face look accidentally angry?
- Can you tweak it just a little – without making it fake?

You're not trying to perform.

You're just making sure the message matches the mood.

🎯 Try This Together: Feelings Without Words

With a partner or group:

- Choose an emotion to act out *only with your face* (no words, no sounds).
- The others guess what you're trying to say.

Then try these challenges:

- Mix two emotions: nervous + excited, tired + happy, annoyed + respectful
- Try "pretending to be fine when you're not"
- Try "caring without looking too obvious"

Talk about what was easy or hard.

This is how actors train – and they get paid to fake feelings. You're just learning how to show your real ones more clearly.

◆ **You Don't Owe Everyone a Smile – But You Should Know What You're Sending Out**

You don't have to walk around grinning like you're in a toothpaste commercial.

But if your neutral face comes off cold, bored, or sarcastic, it's helpful to know that – and **decide when to shift it.**

That's not fake. That's skill.

✏️ Flip the Script: When My Face Got Me in Trouble

Think of a time you got called out for your "look" when you didn't mean anything by it.

Write or reflect:

- What were you actually feeling?
- What might your face have looked like?
- What could you do next time to show what you *actually* meant?

Now practice your version of "neutral but chill."

Soft eyes. Relaxed mouth. Gentle eyebrows. Not fake – just clear.

What to Remember:

- Your face speaks before you do – so learn what it's saying
- "This is just my face" may be true, but it still sends a message
- You don't have to smile, but you *can* make small shifts when it counts
- Adjusting your expression is like tuning an instrument – not pretending, just getting in sync

Mini Reality Check: Yes, This Is Unfair

It *is* annoying to get judged for your face.

It *is* frustrating when people assume things based on a look.

But you can either fight the world every day…

or learn the signals and make them work for you.

That's not losing.

That's strategy.

Chapter 3:
Tone, Volume, and the Magical Skill of Not Sounding Rude When You're Not

You've probably heard it before:

- "Don't talk to me like that."
- "You need to watch your tone."
- "It's not what you said, it's *how* you said it."

And you're thinking,

I literally just said okay.

I wasn't being rude.

That's just how I talk.

Sound familiar?

Welcome to the world of **tone**, where your voice can get you in trouble *even when your words are perfectly fine.*

◆ What Is "Tone," Really?

Tone is the emotion your voice sends out, whether you mean to or not.

Your tone includes:

- **Pitch** – high or low
- **Speed** – fast, slow, choppy
- **Volume** – loud, soft, whisper-shouting
- **Energy** – flat, enthusiastic, tense
- **Edge** – a sharpness that makes people think you're being mean, sarcastic, or defensive

The worst part?

You might not notice it at all – but everyone else does.

◆ Why This Happens (and Why It's Worse When You're a Teen)

When you're tired, stressed, trying to explain yourself, or just emotionally maxed out, your tone gets... spiky.

You might sound:

- Rude
- Bored
- Defensive
- Mocking
- Like you're about to fight someone (even if you're just saying "I don't know")

And because you're a teenager? Adults are **already** watching for tone.

Unfair? Yep.

But knowing how to control it = power.

- **You're Not a Robot – But You Can Adjust the Dials**

This isn't about faking enthusiasm or never sounding annoyed.

It's about learning to **match your tone to your intention** – so people actually hear what you *mean*, not just how you sound.

🛠 Try This: Tone Shift Practice (Solo)

Pick one short sentence:

- "I didn't mean it like that."
- "Okay."
- "I don't know."
- "Can I go now?"
- "Sure."

Now say it:

1. With a calm, respectful tone
2. With an annoyed tone
3. With a bored or flat tone
4. With sarcastic energy
5. With "I'm trying really hard to sound okay" tone

Listen to yourself or record it.

You'll be surprised how much emotion leaks out – even when you're "just saying the words."

🎯 Try This Together: Tone Detective

In a group or with a partner:

1. One person says a phrase in a chosen tone (without naming it)
2. The others guess the mood or message behind it
3. Discuss: Was the tone clear? Was it misunderstood?

Now flip it: say the exact same words *intentionally wrong* – like "I'm sorry" in a rude tone – and talk about what happens.

This shows how powerful (and dangerous) tone can be.

Quick Tip: Use a Tone Reset Phrase

If you get called out for your tone but didn't mean it that way, try:

- "Sorry, I didn't mean it to sound like that. Let me try again."
- "I'm not mad, I'm just overwhelmed."
- "I really didn't mean to sound rude. I just said it fast."

This tells the other person:

I care enough to fix it.

You don't have to agree that they're right – you're just resetting the vibe.

Flip the Script: The Time My Voice Betrayed Me

Think of a time you said something and someone got mad – even though you thought your words were fine.

Write or reflect:

- What were you actually feeling?
- What did they think you were feeling?
- What could you try differently next time – tone, speed, volume?

Bonus: Try saying it again now, out loud, in a calmer tone. Feels better, right?

☑ **What to Remember**

- Your tone changes how people hear you – even if your words are perfect
- You can sound rude without meaning to (and kind without overdoing it)
- Learning to shift tone is not fake – it's clarity
- A calm tone opens doors. A sharp one shuts them – even if you're right.

Mini Reality Check: You Don't Owe People a Smile, But You Might Owe Them a Softer Voice

People will say "don't take that tone with me."

What they really mean is:

"I feel like you're mad, disrespectful, or don't care."

If that's not what you meant?

Change the tone. Keep the point.

That's how you stay in control of the conversation *and* your reputation.

Chapter 4:
Texts, Chats, and Social Media – Soft Skills Go Digital

You send a text.

Just one little message:

"ok."

And then... the vibe changes.

They're distant. Cold. Typing bubbles... then nothing.

Now you're wondering: *Did I do something wrong?*

Welcome to **digital communication**, where people misunderstand each other **faster than you can type "nvm."**

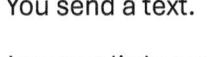 **Tone Doesn't Travel Well**

In real life, people hear your voice, see your face, watch your body language.

Online? All they get are your words.

And maybe your emoji game.

Which means:

- "What are you doing?" can sound like "I'm curious" or "I'm annoyed"
- "K" can sound like "cool" or "I'm mad at you"
- "Sure." can feel like an eye-roll – even if you didn't mean it that way

In text, people **fill in the emotion themselves** – and they often get it wrong.

- **Why This Matters More Than You Think**

So what if someone reads your tone wrong?

Well, that's how:
- Group chats fall apart
- People get excluded without knowing why
- Friendships cool off
- You lose trust without ever getting a chance to explain

Digital drama often starts with a **soft skills misfire** – not bad intentions.

But you can fix that.

📌 Some Text Habits That Confuse People

Here are a few digital behaviors that can send mixed signals:

Some Text Habits That Confuse People

1. Typing short, fast replies

    What you meant: "I'm in a hurry"

    What they might hear: "I'm annoyed with you"

2. No punctuation

    What you meant: "I'm casual"

    What they might hear: "I'm cold or careless"

3. Too much punctuation (!!!)

    What you meant: "I'm excited!"

    What they might hear: "I'm overdoing it and it's weird"

4. Dry responses ("K", "fine")

    What you meant: "I'm tired"

    What they might hear: "You just got on my last nerve"

5. Long pause, then short reply

    What you meant: "I was busy"

    What they might hear: "I don't want to talk to you"

🛠 Try This: Text Translation Challenge

Take a simple sentence like:

- "I guess so."
- "That's fine."
- "You can do what you want."
- "Whatever."
- "I'm not mad."

Now read them in your head *two ways*:

1. Calm, friendly
2. Distant, cold, or passive-aggressive

Same words, completely different vibe.

That's the danger – and power – of tone in writing.

Now rewrite each one to be **clearer and kinder**, if that's what you actually meant.

Example:

- "I guess so." → "I think so – I'm not 100% sure, though."
- "Whatever." → "It's cool, I'll go with whatever you want."

🎯 Try This Together: Group Chat Decoder

With a friend or group, pull up a (non-personal) chat message or mock one up.

Guess:

- What did the sender *probably* mean?
- How could someone else *misread* it?
- How could they rephrase it for clarity?

This helps build the skill of *editing for tone* – which most adults still don't know how to do.

💡 Quick Tip: Emoji & Punctuation Are Tools – Use Them Thoughtfully

You don't need to fill every sentence with hearts and smiley faces, but using nothing can sound harsh, too.

Compare:

- "sure" vs. "sure!" vs. "sure :)"
- "fine." vs. "fine lol"
- "ok" vs. "ok!!" vs. "ok..."

Pick the version that matches your actual mood.

Not to please people, but to stop misunderstandings before they start.

✏️ Flip the Script: The Text That Went Wrong

Think of a time you sent a message that got misunderstood.

Maybe someone got mad, didn't reply, or called you out.

Write or reflect:

- What did you send?
- What do you think they thought it meant?
- How would you say it differently now?

Bonus: Practice writing a "tone reset" message – something like:

"Hey – I didn't mean that to sound harsh earlier. Sorry if it came off wrong."

✅ **What to Remember:**

- Your words online are missing body language and tone – so people guess.
- Tiny things (punctuation, emoji, timing) can change how messages are received.
- If something feels weird in a chat? It probably does to them too.
- Clarity is kindness. It helps people feel safe with you.

🔋 **Mini Digital Reality Check: You Don't Have to Respond Right Away – But You Do Have to Communicate**

It's okay to need a break from texting.

It's okay to ghost a toxic conversation.

But if you care about someone and want to keep their trust, say something like:

"Hey – I'm not ignoring you. I just need some space today."

That's not extra. That's maturity.

And trust me, people notice.

Chapter 5: Apologizing Like a Real Person (Not a Scripted Robot)

You messed up.

You said something, did something, forgot something.

Now someone's upset and you're stuck with that awful feeling:

Do I say sorry? What if it makes it worse?

What if I don't actually think I did anything wrong?

Here's the truth:

Apologies aren't about losing.

They're about **resetting the relationship**.

◆ Why Apologizing Is So Weird

Apologizing feels risky because it means:
- Admitting you caused a problem (even by accident)
- Facing someone's anger or hurt
- Being vulnerable (ugh, emotions)
- Possibly not getting forgiven (that part hurts)

But skipping the apology doesn't make the problem go away.

It just **cements the damage** – and makes people trust you less.

◆ **Intent vs. Impact (Again)**

You might not have *meant* to hurt someone.

You might think they're being *too sensitive*.

You might not agree with why they're upset.

But here's what matters more:

They were hurt.

And you were involved.

That's enough to acknowledge it.

Apologizing doesn't always mean "I was wrong."

It can mean:

- "I get that this landed badly."
- "I care about how this affected you."
- "I don't want this to sit between us."

That's maturity. Not weakness.

☑ What a Real Apology Looks Like

A solid apology usually has these parts:

1. **Acknowledgment** – "I get that what I said upset you."
2. **Ownership** – "I said it too fast and didn't think."
3. **Optional context** – "I wasn't trying to hurt you."
4. **Reconnection** – "I want to fix this if you're open to it."

Things to skip:
- "I'm sorry you feel that way."
- "I didn't mean to, but…"
- "I'm sorry, but you also – "
- Any version of "You're being dramatic."

You don't have to agree with their reaction.

You just have to respect that it *happened*.

🛠 Try This: Rewrite the Auto-Apology (Solo Practice)

Take a fake apology like:

- "Sorry, okay? Jeez."
- "I said sorry already."
- "Whatever, I didn't mean it like that."

Now rewrite it as if you actually care about fixing things:

Examples:

- "I didn't realize how that came off. I'm sorry it landed that way."
- "I was frustrated, but I know I crossed a line. That's on me."
- "That wasn't what I meant at all, but I see why you're upset. I'm sorry."

Practice saying them out loud.

Yes, it'll feel awkward. Yes, it'll also make you better.

🎯 Try This Together: Apology Role-Play

In a group or with a partner, practice these low-stakes scenarios:
- You took someone's spot in line
- You snapped at someone while tired
- You forgot to include someone in a group invite
- You made a joke that didn't land well

Try apologizing two ways:
1. Defensive or dismissive
2. Calm and sincere

Talk about what each version felt like on both sides.

Spoiler: the sincere one always wins.

💡 Quick Tip: You Can Apologize Without Being a Doormat

Saying sorry doesn't mean you're trash.

It means you're tuned in.

You can still stand your ground, set boundaries, or explain yourself later.

But leading with "I see where I went wrong" opens the door for people to meet you halfway.

And that's often all it takes.

🔧 Flip the Script: The One I Wish I Handled Better

Think of a time you *could have* apologized, but didn't.

Or you tried – but it came out wrong.

Or you didn't realize someone was hurt until later.

Reflect or write:

- What happened?
- What do you think they needed to hear?
- What could you say now that might still help?

You don't have to say it *to them* right away.

Start by saying it *to yourself* with honesty.

✅ What to Remember:

- Apologizing isn't about losing – it's about repairing trust

- You don't need to agree with someone's feelings to respect them
- A good apology is short, clear, and *human*
- "I'm sorry" isn't weakness – it's strength that makes relationships stronger

🔋 Mini Reality Check: Most People Don't Remember the Mistake – They Remember the Recovery

They remember how you acted after.

Did you:

- Deny it?
- Defend it?
- Disappear?

Or did you own it and try to make it right?

That's what makes people trust you again.

That's what earns respect.

And that's what makes *you* feel better, too.

Chapter 6: Group Work, Teachers, and Being Assertive Without Being a Problem

You've been there.

The group project.

One person tries to do everything.

Another disappears.

One has zero clue what's going on.

And you? You're somewhere between *"I got this"* and *"Don't make me carry you."*

Or maybe it's a different scene:

You're confused in class.

You want help.

But every time you raise your hand, you feel judged – or worse, ignored.

Welcome to the tightrope of **being assertive without being "extra."**

◆ What's the Difference Between Assertive and Aggressive?

Aggressive = loud, forceful, demanding, dismissive of others

Assertive = clear, respectful, direct, confident

Assertive means:

- You ask for what you need without apologizing for existing
- You disagree respectfully without starting drama
- You take up space without pushing other people out

This is one of the most powerful soft skills you can learn – because it makes you someone people *listen to*.

◆ Group Work: The Social Obstacle Course

Here's why group work is tough:

- You didn't choose the group
- You don't control the roles
- You're being judged by other people's effort

It's unfair – but you *can* make it better by:

- Communicating your role early
- Calling people in – not out
- Speaking up without sounding like you're accusing everyone of being lazy

🛠 Try This: Group Work Scripts

Scenario 1: You're doing everything.

Default response: "Ugh, no one's helping. I guess I'll just do it."

Assertive version: "Hey, can we divide this up so we each have a piece? I'm feeling swamped."

Scenario 2: Someone won't stop dominating.

Default response: *Silently rage until you snap.*

Assertive version: "I think we're all supposed to contribute here – can I share my part?"

Scenario 3: You disagree with the plan.

Default response: "Whatever. I don't care."

Assertive version: "Can I suggest something different? I think it might work better."

You're not being bossy. You're being part of a team – *and teams need voices.*

- **Dealing With Teachers Without Spiraling**

You're allowed to:
- Ask questions
- Ask for help
- Ask for time
- Ask for respect

Even from teachers.

But how you ask makes all the difference.

🛠 Try This: Help Requests That Actually Work

Instead of:

- "This makes no sense."
- "You didn't explain it right."
- "Do we *have* to do this?"

Try:

- "I'm having trouble with part of this – can we go over it again?"
- "I think I missed the part where you explained ___. Could you go back for a sec?"
- "Can I ask for help without slowing everyone down?"

You don't need to be perfect. Just polite, clear, and grounded.

Most teachers want to help – you just have to give them something to work with.

◎ Try This Together: Assertiveness Challenge

In a pair or small group, take turns with these role-play starters:

- You need someone to stop interrupting you
- You need to ask for help before a test
- You need to tell someone their idea won't work (without being rude)
- You need to set a boundary like: "Please don't talk about me like that"

The goal isn't to "win" – it's to say what you mean in a way people can hear.

Then talk about it:

- What felt awkward?
- What worked better than expected?
- How can you say something strong *without sounding like a jerk*?

Quick Tip: Use the "I + Feel + Because" Formula

This soft-skill sentence starter works like magic:

- "I feel overwhelmed because I'm doing the whole project."
- "I feel frustrated because I'm confused and don't know how to ask."
- "I feel ignored because I've tried speaking up but nothing's changed."

It's clear. It's respectful. And it's hard to argue with feelings.

(That doesn't mean they'll always agree – but they'll usually listen.)

Flip the Script: The Time I Should've Spoken Up

Think of a time you wanted to say something – to a group or teacher – but didn't.

Write or reflect:

- What stopped you?
- What were you afraid would happen?
- What could you say next time that would feel brave *and* respectful?

You don't have to be loud.

You just have to speak.

✅ What to Remember:

- Assertiveness is not the same as being loud or bossy
- You can be direct without being aggressive
- Good group communication = less drama, more results
- Teachers are human. Help them help you. Ask clearly, calmly, and with purpose.

🔋 Mini Reality Check: You're Allowed to Advocate for Yourself

Needing help isn't annoying.

Asking for support doesn't make you weak.

Suggesting a different idea isn't disrespectful.

Soft skills give you **the language** to make your needs known *without making enemies.*

That's power.

Use it.

📖 **Chapter 7:
Social Rules That Aren't
in the Handbook**

Some rules are written down.

Raise your hand. Don't run in the halls. Show your work.

But **most** of the rules – the ones that matter most in social life – are silent.

Nobody teaches them.

You're just supposed to magically know:

- When to stop talking
- When someone's fake laughing
- When "it's fine" actually means *it's absolutely not fine*

Welcome to the world of **unwritten social rules**.

It's confusing, unfair, and *completely survivable* – once you know what to look for.

◆ What Are "Unspoken Rules," Anyway?

They're the social expectations people follow *without saying them out loud*.

Like:

- Don't stand too close
- Don't interrupt a group mid-convo
- Don't say "actually…" every time someone gets something wrong
- Don't overshare in the first five minutes of meeting someone
- Don't keep texting if someone gives dry replies every time

Nobody writes these rules down.

But if you break them, people notice.

So this chapter gives you **decoder glasses**.

How to Spot a Social Cue (Before It Becomes a Problem)

A social cue is a sign someone gives – through:
- Body language (shifting, turning away, crossing arms)
- Facial expression (tight smile, blank stare, raised brow)
- Tone (flat voice, one-word answers)
- Timing (long pauses, slow responses, lack of follow-up)

It often means:
- "You're talking too long"
- "I want to leave this convo"
- "That joke didn't land"
- "I'm uncomfortable but not saying it out loud"

It's not about reading minds. It's about reading the **room**.

🛠 Try This: Cue Catcher Practice

Think of a time someone got quiet or pulled back in a conversation. Try to answer these:

- What changed about their body or face?
- Did their voice sound different?
- Did you push through – or change gears?

Now practice this awareness in real time:

- Watch for crossed arms, head tilts, or shifting feet
- Notice if replies get shorter or tones get flatter
- Then ask yourself: *Should I pause here? Change topics? Check in?*

That's not people-pleasing. That's **situational awareness**.

💡 A Quick Word on Side-Eye and Subtweets

In teen life, not all social cues are subtle.

Sometimes you get:
- The Look™
- An obvious whisper
- A group chat cold front
- A social media post that feels... *directed at you*

Here's the trick: you don't have to assume guilt *just because someone's being weird.*

If you're unsure, try:
- "Hey, I noticed things felt off – are we good?"
- "I saw that post – if it's about me, I'd rather talk than guess."
- "I might've said something weird earlier. If I did, tell me."

You're not being dramatic. You're **clearing the air like a pro.**

🎯 Try This Together: Decode the Scene

Create or act out mini-skits in a group:

- One person breaks a hidden social rule
- The others react with nonverbal cues

Then stop and discuss:

- What was the unspoken rule?
- What were the signals it had been broken?
- How could the speaker have picked up on that earlier?

This builds real-world reaction time.

And it makes you *that person* who just "gets it" – without guessing.

💡 Quick Tip: You Can Always Ask (Politely)

If someone gives you weird vibes, and you're not sure why, try:

- "Did I say something wrong just now?"
- "You got really quiet – are we good?"
- "I'm not always great at picking up on stuff like this, but I want to be respectful."

That kind of honesty?

It's rare.

And incredibly respected.

✍️ Flip the Script: That Moment Went Weird

Think of a conversation that got awkward, and you weren't sure why.

Reflect or write:

- What were the unspoken rules at play?
- Did you miss a signal?
- Could you have said something differently – or just checked in?

This doesn't mean you were wrong. It just helps you be **ready next time.**

☑ **What to Remember:**
- Most social rules aren't taught – but you *can* learn them
- Body language, tone, and timing are full of useful signals
- It's okay to miss a cue. It's not okay to ignore them over and over
- Awareness beats perfection every time

🔋 Mini Reality Check: Knowing the Rules Doesn't Mean You Have to Follow Them All

You don't have to obey every social rule.

You just need to know *what the consequences are if you don't.*

And then decide.

Want to go off-script? Do it boldly.

But if you want to stay connected, respected, and understood?

You'll need to learn how the game works first.

And you're doing that right now.

Chapter 8:
Emotional Self-Control
(Without Going Numb or Exploding)

Sometimes you're totally fine.

And sometimes… you're **one sideways comment away from flipping a desk.**

You're not dramatic.

You're not unstable.

You're just **a human with emotions** – and a brain that's still wiring itself up.

But here's the thing:

In school, with friends, at work, **how you handle your emotions matters**.

People don't always care why you're upset.

They just remember **how you acted** when you were.

And that's why emotional self-control is such a power move.

- **Self-Control ≠ No Emotions**

Let's get this straight:

- Self-control does **not** mean being emotionless
- It does **not** mean smiling when you're angry
- It does **not** mean bottling everything up until you explode later

It means:

- Knowing *when* to express something
- Knowing *how* to express it
- Knowing how to pause before saying or doing something you regret

It's not about being fake.

It's about being **strategic with your feelings**.

◆ The Moment Before the Meltdown

You probably know the signs:

- Breathing changes
- Shoulders tighten
- Your chest gets hot or heavy
- Everything someone says suddenly sounds annoying
- You want to cry or punch something – or both

This is where the **real soft skill** comes in.

Because what you do **in the moment** can either:

- Blow things up
- Shut you down
- Or help you take a second to think and stay in control

Let's aim for that third one.

🛠 Try This: The Pause Button

Next time you feel yourself getting overwhelmed, try these steps:

1. Notice the signal.

"I feel tight. I'm clenching. I want to yell."

2. Name the emotion.

"I'm embarrassed."

"I'm angry."

"I feel disrespected."

3. Pick a strategy.

- Take 3 slow breaths
- Say, "Can we take a break?"
- Ask, "Can we come back to this?"
- Look down at something (your hands, a paper) to avoid reacting immediately

This sounds small – but it can **completely change the outcome** of a conversation.

🎯 Try This Together: Recovery Role-Play

In a group or pair, act out emotional flashpoints like:

- Being accused of something you didn't do
- Being interrupted over and over
- Being called "too sensitive"
- Someone rolling their eyes at your opinion

Now try **three versions** of your response:

1. Total emotional takeover (yelling, snapping, storming out)
2. Shutting down (silent treatment, freezing, leaving the convo)
3. Controlled response ("I need a second." / "That upset me. Can we pause?")

Then talk about what each one would lead to in real life – and which you'd *want* to be known for.

💡 Emotional Control Doesn't Mean Silence

You're allowed to:

- Say, "I'm upset"
- Cry
- Disagree
- Be passionate
- Show frustration

You're just choosing **how** to do it in a way that doesn't hurt your message – or your relationships.

🪶 Flip the Script: The Time I Lost It

Think of a time you totally lost your cool.

Maybe you snapped, cried, shut down, or walked out.

Reflect or write:

- What set you off?
- What were the signs leading up to it?
- What could you try next time to stay grounded – even just 10% longer?

This isn't about shame. It's about having **tools**.

✅ What to Remember:

- You're allowed to feel things deeply – but you *choose* how to express them

- Emotional control is about timing, not erasing your feelings

- The calmest person in the room usually has the most power

- Self-control builds your rep – and your confidence

🔋 Mini Reality Check: You're Not "Too Emotional." You're Learning Emotional Strategy.

Strong emotions mean you care.

They mean you have opinions. Boundaries. Passion. Fire.

And with the right tools, you can show that without burning the place down.

That's real strength.

That's emotional fluency.

That's soft skills at work.

Chapter 9: Being a Decent Human Without Overdoing It

You want to be a good person.

But you also don't want to be the one who:

- Always gives in
- Feels invisible
- Gets walked on
- Or gets called "fake nice" behind your back

So what does it actually mean to be **a decent human** without turning into a pushover, a people-pleaser, or someone you barely recognize?

Let's find out.

- **Kind ≠ Nice All the Time**

"Nice" is polite.

"Nice" can be fake.

"Nice" sometimes smiles while dying inside.

- **Kindness** is different.

Kindness is:

- Noticing when someone's left out
- Checking in when someone seems off
- Giving a real compliment without expecting anything back
- Setting a boundary *without being a jerk about it*

It's quiet power.

It's real empathy.

It's **respect for others and yourself.**

◆ How to Be Kind Without Being a Try-Hard

You don't have to:
- Say yes to everything
- Hug everyone
- Respond to every text immediately
- Be the emotional trash can for people who never check on you

You can be kind **and** say:
- "I'm not free right now."
- "I care about you, but I don't have the energy for that today."
- "That joke makes me uncomfortable."
- "I need some space."

That's not rude. That's **emotionally responsible.**

🛠 Try This: Compliment Challenge (Solo or Group)

Try giving one compliment per day for a week that:

- Isn't about appearance
- Isn't overly dramatic
- Feels genuine

Examples:

- "You ask good questions."
- "I like how you explained that."
- "You're easy to work with."

Then reflect:

- How did it feel to say?
- What reaction did you get?
- Did it change the vibe with that person?

This is a low-risk way to build connection and learn **how powerful kindness can be**.

🎯 Try This Together: Boundary Practice

With a friend or group, act out scenes where someone:

- Keeps asking for help when you're busy
- Starts talking trash and wants you to join in
- Tells you something heavy and expects you to "fix" it
- Invites you to something you really don't want to do

Try these boundary scripts:

- "I want to help, but I'm not the right person for that."
- "I'm not comfortable with that topic."
- "I'm flattered, but I need to sit this one out."
- "I can't carry that right now. You might want to talk to an adult or counselor."

Talk afterward:

- What felt empowering?
- What felt awkward?
- Which one would you actually use?

💡 Quick Tip: You Don't Owe Everyone Your Energy

Kindness is *offered*, not *owed*.

You get to choose:

- Who gets your time
- Who gets your emotional energy
- Who earns your trust

That doesn't make you mean.

It makes you **honest and safe** – for you and for others.

🪶 Flip the Script: When I Gave Too Much

Think of a time you said "yes" when you didn't want to.

Maybe you stayed in a group chat too long. Took on work that stressed you. Listened when you were emotionally drained.

Write or reflect:

- Why did you say yes?
- What happened because of it?
- What could you say next time that honors both you and them?

That's how you **build kindness with boundaries.**

☑ **What to Remember:**

- Kindness isn't weakness – it's a choice backed by awareness
- You can care about people without carrying them
- Saying no can be respectful
- Setting boundaries isn't mean – it's maturity

🔋 Mini Reality Check: You Don't Need to Prove You're a Good Person Every Second of the Day

You're allowed to:

- Log off
- Be quiet
- Say no
- Pick yourself
- Walk away from energy vampires

You're still a good person.

Sometimes even a *better* one – because you know your limits.

Chapter 10:
Soft Skills at Work
(or Work-Like Places)

Let's be real: your first job is probably not your dream job.

It might be:

- Bagging groceries
- Taking orders
- Babysitting
- Working at a summer camp
- Running tech for a school event
- Volunteering at a community thing your mom signed you up for

Doesn't matter.

Because the skills you bring to that first job – or volunteer gig or internship – **go with you** into every opportunity after.

And if you use your soft skills right?

People notice. And doors open.

◆ Why Workplaces Don't Just Care About Skills

Your boss cares about more than just whether you can do the thing.

They also care about:
- Whether you show up on time
- Whether you're easy to work with
- Whether you're teachable
- Whether customers trust you
- Whether you make problems bigger or smaller

That's not about your job title. That's your **soft skills in action**.

◆ How to Look Reliable (Even If You Feel Totally New)

You don't have to fake confidence.

You just have to show:

- **Curiosity** – Ask good questions
- **Clarity** – Confirm tasks instead of guessing
- **Responsibility** – Own your mistakes and follow through
- **Awareness** – Don't make people chase you down or repeat instructions

Bonus points for:

- Remembering people's names
- Saying "I've got that" or "Can I help with something else?"
- Keeping your phone away unless it's part of the job

That alone puts you ahead of half the competition.

✸ Try This: Workplace Decoder (Solo Practice)

Answer honestly:

- What's one thing that would make you trust someone at work?
- What's one thing that makes someone look unreliable, fast?
- If you were the manager, what kind of behavior would impress you?
- Now – do you do those things?

If not, no shame. But now you know what to aim for.

🎯 Try This Together: Role-Play the Real World

In a group or pair, act out these situations:

- A customer is frustrated – you're not sure why
- You made a mistake but aren't sure if you should admit it
- A coworker is slacking and you're picking up the slack
- You don't understand the task but feel awkward asking again

Then switch:

- How would you handle it as the employee?
- As the manager?
- What soft skill would help in each case?

This shows how **tiny decisions** can build – or ruin – your reputation fast.

💡 Quick Tip: Always Say This One Line

If you don't know what to do or you're overwhelmed, say:

"Can you show me once more so I get it right?"

This line = responsible, teachable, trustworthy.

No one expects you to know everything. But they do expect you to *want to learn*.

✏️ Flip the Script: When I Made It Worse

Think of a time when a work-like task went off the rails – school project, chore, event, anything with expectations.

Write or reflect:

- What happened?
- What was your response – emotionally and socially?
- What soft skill could've helped?
- What would you try next time?

That's how you build your "work" self: one choice at a time.

☑ What to Remember:

- Your first jobs are more about **how** you work than what you're doing
- Soft skills = respect, trust, clarity, consistency
- You don't have to be perfect – you just have to be *learning*
- Every situation is practice for something bigger

🔋 Mini Reality Check: The People Who Get Promoted Aren't Always the Best at the Job

They're the ones who:

- Stay cool under pressure
- Communicate clearly
- Admit when they need help
- Handle feedback without melting
- Make the room better

And that?

That's soft skills.

That's you – if you want it to be.

Closing Chapter:
You Don't Have to Be a Genius – You Just Have to Be Aware

If you've made it all the way here, pause and take that in.

You've just read a book about how to **understand people, show up stronger, and handle social life without burning out** – and that's a big deal.

Soft skills aren't loud.

They don't come with trophies.

They're not easy to brag about in a group chat.

But they're everywhere.

They're how people decide whether to trust you, hire you, invite you, listen to you, or respect you.

And now? **You've got the tools.**

◆ You Don't Need to Memorize Everything – Just Start Noticing

You don't have to be perfect.

You don't have to control every moment.

You just need to pay attention to things like:

- What your face and voice are doing
- How other people react
- How your words land
- What your tone says when you're not thinking about it
- When to ask, when to pause, when to reset

If you mess up? Cool. Everyone does.

Fix it. Keep going.

Soft Skills Are Like a Superpower – But You Have to Practice

The point of this book wasn't to make you someone else.

It was to help the *real you* come through clearly.

So that when people meet you, work with you, or talk to you – they actually get it.

They see who you are. Not just your tired face. Not just your overwhelmed tone.

You.

Practice one thing at a time.

Use it in school. Online. At work. With friends. With adults.

Build it into your instincts.

You've already started.

💡 You're Not Behind. You're Ahead.

Most people go their whole lives never figuring this stuff out.

You're not "too emotional." You're not "too blunt." You're not "too awkward."

You're learning the skills no one ever taught out loud.

And every time you try – even a little – you're leveling up.

You've got this.

✸ Last Challenge: Pick One Soft Skill to Use Tomorrow

Which will you try first?

- A clearer tone?
- A kinder boundary?
- A better reaction in a group?
- Asking for help without panicking?
- Giving a real apology?
- Reading a vibe before it crashes?

Pick one. Try it.

And remember: you're allowed to take up space *and* still be thoughtful.

That's the power move.

That's what you've learned.

And the best part?

You didn't change.

You just translated.

📖 Glossary: Soft Skills Decoder

Think of this as your cheat sheet for the social stuff people expect you to "just know." These are terms used in this book – now explained, no guessing required.

Body Language
The nonverbal stuff your body says – like posture, facial expression, and gestures. Example: slumped shoulders and crossed arms might say "I don't want to be here," even if you don't say a word.

Boundary
A personal rule you set to protect your energy or feelings. Example: "Please don't yell at me," or "I can't talk about that right now." Boundaries aren't mean – they're healthy.

Masking
When you hide your real emotions or reactions to seem more "normal" or socially acceptable. Like pretending you're not anxious when you really are, or laughing at a joke you didn't find funny.

Passive-Aggressive
Saying something that *sounds* polite but actually has a hidden edge. Like "Sure, whatever" or "No, it's fine. I'm used to being left out." It's a way of showing you're upset without saying it directly.

People-Pleasing
Always saying yes or trying to make everyone happy to avoid conflict – even if it stresses you out. It's not the same as kindness. Kindness has limits. People-pleasing forgets them.

Read the Room
Paying attention to the vibe in the room and adjusting your behavior accordingly. If everyone's quiet and serious, that's probably not the time to go full stand-up comic.

Resting Blank Face (RBF)
Your natural face when you're not doing anything in particular. Some people's neutral face gets misread as annoyed, bored, or angry. It's not your fault – but it's worth being aware of.

Social Battery
Your energy level for being around people. When it's drained, everything feels harder. Some people recharge alone. Others recharge socially. Both are normal.

Social Cue
A small signal (usually not verbal) that tells you how a conversation is going. Could be someone leaning away, going quiet, or glancing at their phone. These cues help you figure out when to stop, shift, or keep going.

Subtle
The opposite of obvious. A subtle reaction is quiet or small – like a tiny eye-roll or a shift in posture. A lot of social signals are subtle, which is why they get missed (and why this book exists).

Teachable
Being open to feedback, willing to learn, and able to take correction without flipping out. Managers, teachers, and teammates love this quality. It's soft-skill gold.

Tone
The emotion behind your words. It's what makes "I'm fine" sound completely *not* fine. People react more to your tone than to your actual words.

Trustworthy
Someone others can rely on. You follow through, stay calm under pressure, and don't cause drama. People trust you not because you're perfect – but because you're consistent.

Vibe
The overall feeling or energy someone gives off – usually without saying much. Vibes come from tone, posture, timing, and reactions. You're sending one whether you mean to or not.

📖 Soft Skills Survival Cheat Sheet (Quick Phrases, Real Strategies)

🗣 How to Sound Confident (Not Pushy)

- "Can I ask a quick question about that?"
- "I'm not sure yet, but I want to understand."
- "I think I see another way – mind if I share it?"
- "I'd like to help, but I don't have the bandwidth right now."
- "That's not really okay with me. Can we try something else?"

🔄 Tone Reset Phrases (When It Came Out Wrong)

- "Sorry, let me rephrase that – didn't mean it like it sounded."
- "That came out more intense than I meant."
- "I'm not upset – I just want to be clear."
- "Can I try saying that again in a better way?"

🙇 When You Mess Up (Apology Starters)

- "I get why that felt off. I didn't mean it that way."
- "I crossed a line – I'm sorry about that."
- "That wasn't what I meant, but I see how it landed."
- "I'm learning to handle stuff better. Thanks for pointing that out."

Texting Tips That Actually Help

- Don't leave dry replies if you care – add clarity or tone ("That works :)")
- Use punctuation or emoji if tone could be misread
- If things feel weird: "Hey – just checking, are we okay?"
- If you need space: "I'll get back to you after I reset. Just need a break."

Kindness Without Overdoing It

- "That was a good answer."
- "You did that really well."
- "I see how hard you're trying."
- "I can't help right now, but I still care."
- "I like working with you."

Setting Boundaries Respectfully

- "I'm not comfortable with that."
- "I don't have the energy to talk about that right now."
- "That's not a joke I'm okay with."
- "Please don't talk to me like that."
- "I can't carry this right now – maybe a teacher or adult can help better."

Asking for Help (Without Panic)

- "I think I misunderstood that. Can you show me again?"
- "I tried it this way, but I'm still confused."
- "Can I get some clarification before I mess this up?"
- "Can we go over that one more time?"

Group Work Power Moves

- "Can we divide this up so no one gets overloaded?"
- "I've got this part – can you take that one?"
- "Can we circle back to make sure we're on track?"
- "I'd like to add an idea – can I jump in?"

Emotional Control Tools (In the Moment)

- Take three breaths. Say nothing. Reset.
- Say: "I need a second." / "Can we pause?"
- Write it down instead of snapping back.
- Ask yourself: *Will this help or just release pressure?*

About the Author

Jennifer Larsen is the author of the *Can't I Just...* book series and founder of the Wayfinder Foundation Inc., a nonprofit focused on helping young people build confidence, life skills, and emotional resilience.

With a background in education, psychology, and leadership, Jennifer writes for teens, parents, and anyone feeling overwhelmed by the mess of growing up. Her work combines real talk, practical advice, and just enough humor to keep it all from feeling like homework.

She lives in Connecticut, avoids mornings whenever possible, and believes most things feel easier when you don't have to face them alone.

Find her books and resources at cantijust.com

You're Doing Better Than You Think.

This book is part of the *Can't I Just...* series — a growing collection of no-nonsense guides for teens (and the grown-ups who care about them). If this one helped, there's more where it came from.

Check out the full teen set:

📖 *Can't I Just Stay in My Room?*
A career guidebook for teens who don't want to talk about it.

📖 *Can't I Just Skip College?*
A practical guide to real-world options beyond a four-year degree.

📖 *Can't I Just Be Like Everyone Else?*
You're holding it! A soft skills survival guide for the socially stressed.

💜 And for the adults in your life:
Can't I Just Help My Kid? —
A warm, honest companion for parents trying to guide without pushing.

New books are released regularly.
Find the full series, free extras,
and educator materials at cantijust.com

www.ingramcontent.com/pod-product-compliance
Lightning Source LLC
Chambersburg PA
CBHW070634030426
42337CB00020B/4011